Self-Realization

The Knowledge of the Absolute

A free rendering of the *Astavakra Gita*, the non-dualistic classic
which has been a perennial favorite and source of ultimate illumination for hermits, renunciates and mystics since Vedic times.

Compiled and Edited

by

Al Drucker

TOWERS

Indian Edition 1995

ISBN: 0-9638449-1-1

Published by:
Sri Sathya Sai Towers Hotels Pvt. Ltd.
3/497, Main Road, Prasanthinilayam- 515 134
Phone: 91-8555-87270,87327
Fax: 91-8555-87302

Printed at:
D.K. Fine Art Press (P) Ltd.
Delhi-110052 (INDIA)
Phone : 091-011-7430113/7143353
Fax : 091-011-3264368/7138265

Acknowledgment – The editor wishes to express his appreciation to his wife Janny DeHoog for her inspiration which originally gave rise to this book, and her thoughtful comments and encouragement which saw it through to completion.

There are those who think that the world exists and that the world is real. There are others who think that the world does not exist and that the world is not real. Rare indeed is that blessed one who does not think, but who is ever calm, abiding in the absolute.

Astavakra

Contents

Foreword

This book recounts the dialogue between King Janaka and the young sage, Astavakra, who taught the king the highest wisdom, the knowledge of the self. The enlightenment of Janaka, as depicted here, took place in very ancient times, many thousands of years ago. These teachings, known as the *Astavakra Gita* or *Astavakra Samhita,* have survived all these countless millennia, because they contain the purest truth that can be expressed in words.

This book has been the favorite of hermits, mystics, yogis, sages and itinerant holy men since ancient times. They would cherish and study and restudy these upwellings on supreme truth. Together with the Upanishads, these teachings are unique in the mystical tradition for their exceptional clarity and unwavering fidelity to truth. They have been passed on from *guru* to disciple as a means for focussing on the absolute. The *Astavakra Samhita* was a great favorite of Ramakrishna, the Bengali saint of the last century, who passed it on to his disciple, Vivekananda. In this present century, Sai Baba, the avatar of this age, has spoken very highly of it to some of his devotees. A version of this ancient text, translated sixty years ago by Swami Nityaswarupananda of the Ramakrishna Mission, has been my steady companion for the past two decades and has served as one of the guides for this present work.

My goal has been to bring the terse style of the ancient prose into free-flowing, easily-understandable modern language, without need for footnotes or explanatory comments, and in a size just right to fit in one's pocket. I left intact the many repetitions of basic ideas, which Astavakra restates in various ways to emphasize their importance.

I was led to these teachings twenty years ago when I first heard Sai Baba speak of the wisdom of the Upanishads and the non-dualistic teachings of some of the great sages, such as Vashishta, Astavakra, Shankara, Ramana and Nisargadatta. Years later, while working on the publication of Sai Baba's *Bhagavad Gita* discourses, I was struck by the great esteem Baba had for Astavakra, whom he mentioned a number of times in his discourses. In this present book, I have opened with the account of the first meeting between Astavakra and Janaka as it was originally told by Sai Baba.

I hope that this little book, filled with the most lofty and potent ideas that have ever been phrased in the human mind, will serve you, dear reader, as it has me, in awakening the yearning to know the highest truth. As taught by all the great teachers who have realized the immortal self, self-knowledge is the ultimate goal of human life. We are told that it is the most important knowledge worth pursuing. For as long as the self remains unknown, nothing is really known. Once the self is known, everything is known.

– Al Drucker, Crestone, Colorado, October 1994

Astavakra Gita

The Knowledge of the Absolute

*I*ntensely yearning to know the highest truth, King Janaka sought all over his vast realm, among some of the most renowned scholars and pundits of the world, for a fully-realized being who had the spiritual power to instruct him in the highest wisdom. He could find none. But King Janaka's pure heart and anguished plea alerted the universal teacher to reveal himself and seek out the king.

One day, a young boy with a severely misshapen body appeared in the royal hall. It was during the time of a convocation called by the king to discuss the highest spiritual wisdom. The boy was obviously very poor and had on only a simple loin cloth. No one knew anything about his qualifications or why he was there, except that he had waited patiently for many days outside the palace walls requesting to be admitted to take part in the spiritual discussions. A kindly old scholar had seen him waiting by the door day after day and had mentioned him to the king. The king sent for the boy. His name was Astavakra, meaning the one with eight bends in his body.

When the assembly of great scholars saw Astavakra enter the hall they all laughed at his crooked appearance. But King Janaka did not laugh. He saw the deep inner peace surrounding Astavakra, and he *saw the great dignity and self-confidence with which this young boy deported himself in such an august gathering. Most of all, the king was profoundly moved by the insightful answers Astavakra gave to all the spiritual questions that were posed to him. King Janaka realized that standing before him was a fully-awakened mahatma, a great soul luminous in wisdom and self-knowledge. Here in this unexpected form, was the true teacher he had been so fervently yearning for, the one who could impart to him the mystical knowledge of how to become free from the bondage of ignorance and illusion and end the cycle of birth and death.*

With great humility, the king implored Astavakra to show him the way to enlightenment. Astavakra told the king that a king's palace was not the right setting for such sacred instruction. He asked the king to divest himself of all his royal paraphernalia, don some simple hermit's cloth and follow him to the forest. They left the royal city far behind and reached the serene surroundings of the forest. There, in a glade, Janaka prostrated to Astavakra and in a reverential tone said to him:

My Lord, please tell me, how does self-realization happen? How is liberation attained? How is the supreme knowledge of the absolute acquired?

*A*stavakra was very pleased with Janaka's one-pointed desire to know the truth. In answer to Janaka's fervent request, Astavakra began his discourse wherein he expounded to Janaka the ultimate truth of the infinite. Astavakra said:

My dear child, if you aspire after liberation turn away from your attraction to the five elements and the objects of the senses. Abandon your attachment to these, as you would shun poison. You are in no way connected with them. Fill yourself with the virtues of forgiveness, kindness, sincerity and contentment. Let these be your nectar, let these be your prime sustenance.

You are not made up of earth, water, fire, air or space. You are not the body. Nor are you the mind. You are not a particular name or form. You are not a member of a particular family or tribe. You are not connected with any nation or culture. You are not in any way related to the things of this world. You are not perceivable by the gross or the subtle senses. You are the witness of all these. You are the immortal self, the universal consciousness.

Once you detach yourself from the body and abide in pure awareness, you become your true self, ever peaceful, eternally happy. To know who you really are is liberation.

Concepts of right or wrong, virtue or vice, doing or enjoying, pleasure or pain are all of the mind. They are not of you. You are the self-luminous one, the one seer of all. You are forever free. Verily this has been your bondage that you have identified yourself as the doer rather than as the seer, the pure witness.

You are that all-pervading consciousness, that supreme bliss upon which this illusory universe has become superimposed, just as in the twilight of dusk, a fearsome snake can mistakenly get superimposed by the mind onto a harmless, neutral rope lying on the ground.

Now, burn down the forest of ignorance which has kept you from knowing your true self. Destroy the black serpent of the ego which has so completely hidden you from yourself that you have forgotten that you are the resplendent, pure, ever-free consciousness, eternally happy.

When you consider yourself to be free then you will surely become free. But if you continue to consider yourself as being bound then you will remain bound. As you think so you become. Think of the infinite and you become the infinite. In truth, you are the infinite. Realize it!

You are the immortal self, the all-pervading witness, perfect, actionless, unattached, desireless, non-dual, ever-aware, self-luminous, unborn and undying, forever immersed in the silence of infinite bliss.

But, my pure, blemishless child, through illusion you have allowed yourself to become involved with the world and you think you are part of it. You think you are the body and so you have become bound. You have been caught in the noose of body-consciousness.

Give up your wrong identifications and illusions! Sever all these false notions with the sword of self-knowledge! Abandon your small-minded belief of being an individual! Identify yourself only with the immutable universal self, the pure non-dual consciousness!

You are not a little body existing in this world. No! It is this world which exists in you! You are the pure spirit which pervades this whole universe and on which this whole universe rests. You are the permanent, formless, unconditioned, unfathomable, omnipresent intelligence.

You are the pure mirror on which this whole world appears as an image. This reflection comprising the world of multiplicity comes and goes, as universes appear and disappear in you, but you the supreme self remain unaffected.

Just as the all-pervading space is both inside and outside a jar, so do you the eternal truth exist within all things and beyond all things. You are the all of it, and you are the beyond. Be happy!

In a sudden blaze of illumination caused by the guru's words, Janaka proclaimed:

O, blessed teacher, I now know I am the spotless, tranquil, pure consciousness. I am beyond this perceived world and all its phenomena. Having renounced the world together with the body, now through your grace I have realized the supreme wisdom of self-knowledge.

All this time I thought I was of this world. For so long I have been fooled by illusion. But now I know I am the immortal self. I alone illumine this body and this universe, because I alone exist.

Just as waves, foam and bubbles are not different from water, so the universe is not in the least different from me. Just as cloth is made up of nothing but thread, so this universe is made up of nothing but the supreme self.

Just as every iota of the sugar that is produced from the sugarcane is pervaded by the juice from which it came, so also every iota of the universe that is produced in me, is permeated by me, through and through.

6

Through ignorance a snake appears where there is only a rope. In the same way, through ignorance, a world appears where there is only the self. The world has no existence of its own. It is an illusion superimposed on truth. It comes about because of ignorance of the self and it disappears with knowledge of the self. It is like the superimposed snake which comes about because of ignorance of the rope and disappears with knowledge of the rope.

Just as a clay pot eventually dissolves back into clay, just as a wave eventually dissolves back into water, just as a gold bracelet eventually dissolves back into gold, so the universe having emanated from me through ignorance, will dissolve back into me with the dawn of self-knowledge. When all the illusory names and forms have disappeared, only I, the supreme self, will remain.

O, how wonderful am I! Adorations to myself, who knows no decay and who survives even the destruction of the world. O, how glorious am I, who though appearing as a body and appearing to be one of countless many, in truth am the one and only one who has ever existed. I have neither come from anywhere nor am I going anywhere. I am forever in the eternal now, abiding in myself.

My very nature is light. I am ever effulgent and splendorous. When this universe manifests itself, it is I alone that shine.

O prostrations to myself, who am nothing that can ever be thought of or spoken of, and yet, who am everything that can ever be thought of or spoken of. I alone bear this universe for all eternity without it ever touching or affecting me.

O, how glorious am I in whom all illusions appear and disappear. In the sleep state, the dreamer, the dream world and the process of dreaming, though appearing to be real, are later seen to be illusory and unreal. So also, in the waking state, the perceiver, that which is perceived and the process of perceiving are all illusory and unreal. I alone am forever real. I alone am that stainless self in which all these illusions appear through ignorance.

The root of all misery is duality. There is no other remedy for this disease except the realization that all objects of experience are unreal and that all there is is the one, pure consciousness and bliss.

Through ignorance I have imposed the limitations of body, mind and world on myself. But now, constantly reflecting on my truth as pure consciousness, I abide in myself, the absolute.

I know neither bondage nor freedom for I am eternally free. With the demise of ignorance, the illusion of the world has lost its basis, and world has ceased to exist. Once the rope is known how can the illusion of the snake appear and be taken seriously?

I know for certain that the body and universe are nothing and the self is pure consciousness alone. Body, heaven and hell, bondage and freedom, as also misery, suffering and fear are all mere imagination. What have I to do will all these, I whose nature is pure consciousness?

O, I do not find any duality. Even though there appears to be a multitude of individual beings I see only my self. Since there is nothing real beside myself to what could I now attach an illusory self?

I am not this body nor do I have a body. I am not this mind nor do I have a mind. I am not the individualized personality nor do I have a personality. Nor am I the ego or the soul. I am pure consciousness. This indeed was my bondage that I had thirsted for life thinking that I would come to an end, and so, I had denied the eternal nature of my self.

O, in me, who am the infinite, limitless ocean, the rising of the wind of the mind produces the multifarious waves of the world. With the calming dawn of knowledge they again vanish without a trace. In me, the boundless ocean, the waves of individual selves with countless names and forms, arise, strike each other, play for a time and disappear, according to their own nature. I the ocean am not affected.

The ego trades in good and bad fruits and acquires profit and loss through endless comings and goings, using the ship of the world to carry on his trade; but unfortunately for it, when the mind disappears and the illusion of the world is destroyed, the ego gets completely obliterated. Such has been my experience.

*A*stavakra *is delighted with Janaka's realization of the ultimate truth. But he wishes to test the extent of Janaka's mental transformation. He challenges Janaka with these words:*

Knowing yourself to be the one indestructible self, how is it that you, being steeped in serenity, still feel attached to acquiring wealth?

How quickly greed shows its vicious head when one mistakes a shiny rock laced with fool's gold for the real thing, due to one's ignorance of the unique luster of pure gold! So also a foolish craving for possessions arises in the deluded one, upon seeing the illusory objects of the world, ignorant as he is of the splendor of the eternal self. But you, having known yourself to be that one supreme totality in which the universe appears like waves on the ocean, why do you still run about like a miserable wretch?

After knowing yourself to be pure consciousness and unsurpassingly beautiful, how can you still be attached to sensual objects and allow yourself to be made impure? It is strange that you who are abiding in the supreme non-duality and intent on liberation should still be subject to lust, and allow yourself to continue to be weakened by amorous pastimes! When you know lust to be an enemy of knowledge, when you are approaching your last days with your vitality ebbing away day by day, strange that you should still be eager for sensual enjoyment!

With whom can we compare that great-souled one who is content with self-knowledge and does not even thirst for liberation? Feasted or tormented, the serene man of knowledge sees only the absolute self and remains steeped in peace, never thirsting for sense-gratification or feeling anger. But you who have understood the ultimate truth and who feel indifferent to the actions of even your own body, witnessing it as if it were another's, how can you still be affected by praise or blame?

Once you, the steady-minded one, know the objects of perception to be worthless, how can you still consider one thing acceptable and another unacceptable? When you have given up worldly attachments and purged your mind of all desires, when you are beyond the pairs of opposites and view all experiences with equal indifference, seeing them as mere happenings that arise as a matter of course, how can you still hanker after pleasure or run away from pain?

Realizing this universe to be a mere illusion and having lost your curiosity about it, how can you, who have attained a steady mind, fear the approach of death?

Janaka calmly responds to Astavakra's challenge:

O illumined master! The knower of the self who is ever conscious of his truth, plays the game of life in the world but is untouched by it. How can he be compared with the ignorant worldly man who is beset with attachments like a deluded beast of burden?

The man of self-knowledge abides effortlessly in that serene, contented state which is his true nature, feeling no pangs of desire or yearning, while even the heavenly hosts unhappily pine for the experience of that exalted state.

How can the heart of one who has known the eternal self ever be touched by virtue or vice? He is like the sky which is not affected by the clouds that appear to darken it or by the rainbow which appears to beautify it.

That great-souled one who has known the entire universe to be the self alone, will always act spontaneously and naturally, without any trace of desire. Fearlessly, he does what is worth doing without concern for praise or blame.

Of all created beings, from the lowest clump of grass to the highest celestial being, the wise one alone acts without desire or aversion. Blessed indeed is that rare enlightened one who always abides in the absolute, and knows the supreme self to be all there ever was and is.

Upon hearing the depth of Janaka's understanding, Astavakra guides Janaka towards the ultimate dissolution of his illusory individuality:

You, the supreme self, are totally unattached. You are free from contact with anything whatsoever. Since your eternal state of being is absolutely pure and free, what is there to renounce? Disidentify yourself with this false individual self. Destroy your identification with the body-complex, and thereby enter into the state of dissolution.

In you, the supreme self, universes arise like insignificant bubbles arising from the vast ocean. Knowing yourself to be the totality of the vast ocean, forever one, give up your identification with this momentary bubble and enter into the state of dissolution, abiding in the absolute.

Knowing the universe to be unreal, having superimposed itself on you like the illusory snake on the rope, how can it truly exist in you who are pure? The universe is merely a mirage, an illusion perceived by the senses. It has no relationship to you. Knowing this, give up all vestige of body-consciousness and enter into the state of dissolution.

You, the absolute self, are perfect. You are forever untouched by misery or happiness, hope or despair, life or death, or any of life's vicissitudes and pairs of opposites. Knowing that you are ever the same and unaffected, pure and incorruptible, relinquish all identification with this individual self and enter into the state of dissolution.

From the depth of his being, Janaka exclaimed:

Boundless am I! I am like the unlimited space in which the phenomenal world is just a little pot, surrounded and permeated by me. I am like the vast ocean in which the universe is a small wave playing in me. I am like the never-ending desert in which the universe is a mirage, projecting illusory images in me. I am the one substratum underlying all existence. I am in all beings and all beings are in me. Knowing myself to be the infinite, the absolute, where is the need to renounce the world, or to accept or destroy it?

14

In me, the boundless ocean, the ship of the universe is tossed hither and thither, impelled by the wind of its own illusory nature. How can I the eternally real be affected by that which is inherently unreal?

In me, the limitless ocean, the wave of the world rises or vanishes of itself. I neither increase nor decrease thereby. In me, the boundless ocean of eternity, the universe is just a fleeting appearance. It has the momentary fascination of a juggler's show but it portents nothing. I remain unattached, ever tranquil and formless. I abide in my serenity.

I who am all-pervasive and infinite can never be limited. How can I be contained by a body, a mind, or by the objects of the world? I who am ever stainless and free from attachment and desire, how can there be any thought of rejection or acceptance in me? I am consciousness itself. I abide in my peacefulness.

To firmly stabilize Janaka in his realization of the self, Astavakra summarizes the steps and pitfalls on the path to liberation and inner peace:

It is bondage when the mind desires or grieves for anything, rejects or accepts anything, or feels happy or angry with anything. Liberation is attained when the mind is free of desire or grief or rejection or acceptance or judgment or anger or happiness.

It is bondage when the mind is attached to anything perceivable by the senses. It is liberation when the mind is detached from all sensory experiences. Knowing this, refrain from accepting or rejecting anything.

When there is no self-identification with the personal 'I', there is liberation; when there is the false identification with the ego-self, there is bondage. Knowing this, give up all sense of yourself as a limited individual, and your truth will reveal itself.

Realize the world to be unreal and renounce your identification with it. Know that all pairs of opposites like joy and sorrow, success and failure, good and evil, worldly and spiritual duties done and not done, are all of this illusory world, and will cease after awakening.

Rare indeed, my child, is that blessed person whose desire for life, enjoyment and learning have been extinguished by observing the misery of others caught in duality and lost in the maze of worldly existence. Realizing the futility of worldly life, be desireless and intent on renunciation, through complete indifference to the world.

The wise man becomes calm by realizing that all worldly accomplishments and aspirations are wiped away by the threefold misery: the suffering caused by physical and mental disease, the suffering caused by inanimate or animate beings and objects, and the suffering caused by natural calamities and upheavals.

Realizing that all craving for worldly results is futile and worthless, reject all such paltry undertakings; they are but transient and insubstantial. Has there ever been a time or an age in which the pairs of opposites, and the resulting bondage due to desires and repulsions, have not existed in men? Quit all these foolish pursuits and be content with what comes of itself. That way you will surely attain perfection.

Having observed the diversity of opinions between the different religious schools of philosophy and among the great seers, saints and *yogis*, become completely indifferent to the pursuit of scholarly knowledge and spiritual practices and immerse yourself in quietude.

He who gains knowledge of the true nature of pure consciousness by cultivating an equanimous mind and becoming completely indifferent to the world, saves himself from the round of births and rebirths. Is such a blessed one not the real spiritual guide?

17

Know that all the objects of the world which you have been craving for, are but combinations and modifications of the five elements. Whether you consider them beautiful or ugly, whether you desire them or dislike them, all phenomenal things are made up of the same stuff, the impermanent five elements. The moment you realize all things to be the same, that they are all evanescent and worthless, unrelated to you the eternal, you will renounce your desires for them and become free from bondage, henceforth abiding only in your true self.

Desires alone make up the world. Therefore, renounce them all. Renunciation of desire and renunciation of the world are exactly the same. Once you are steeped in renunciation you can live anywhere, unaffected by circumstances.

Look upon friends, lands, wealth, houses, wives, presents, and other such marks of good fortune as a dream or a juggler's show, lasting only a few moments. Cultivate indifference to everything worldly. Know that the three goals of life that preoccupy the ordinary man, must be completely expunged in you before you can realize the supreme goal of life: self-knowledge and liberation. Those three goals of ordinary life, namely desire for kith and kin and sensual enjoyments, the achievement of worldly rewards and prosperity, and attainment of a reputation for performing good works, are your enemies; they are attended by mischief and misery.

Know that wherever there is desire there is the world. Desire is bondage and destruction of desire is liberation. Only by non-attachment to the world will you attain the constant joy of the realization of the self. Cloaking yourself in firm dispassion, go beyond desire and be happy.

You are the one pure intelligence. The universe is devoid of intelligence and is unreal. It is the child of ignorance. Pursuing the knowledge of things of the world is only a way of further delving into ignorance. What is the use of knowing that which is unreal? What can you yet desire to know except the eternal self? When that is known everything is known, and when that is not known, nothing is known.

Kingdoms, sons, wives, bodies, and pleasures have all been lost to you birth after birth, even though you were attached to them. Enough of prosperity, desires, and pious deeds! The mind did not find repose in these in the dreary forest of the world.

For how many births have you not done hard and painful work with body, mind, and speech? Have they given you any lasting happiness? Why continue in worldly actions which spring from ignorance and only cause bondage and misery? Cease all these foolish pursuits, at least from today.

He who has realized that change and destruction is in the very nature of things, finds repose in spirit, remaining ever unperturbed and free from pain. He who has known for certain that the universe has arisen from the self, exists in the self and dissolves in the self, and that there is no existence other than the self, becomes peaceful with all his desires set at rest. He will not be attached to anything whatsoever.

He who knows for certain that happiness and misery, birth and death are due to the effects of past actions, does not find anything to accomplish. Thus, he becomes free from care and remains unattached even though engaged in action, for he knows he is not the doer. He who has known for certain that his present life with all its vicissitudes is the result of his past actions, and that adversity and prosperity come in their own time through the effects of *karma*, is ever contented and unaffected by changes in fortune.

He who has realized that it is the identification of the mind with worldly objects that breeds attachment and gives rise to misery in this world, becomes free from it. He is forever happy, peaceful, and rid of desires that are due to caring for things of the world. Being unattracted to worldly things, the high-souled one has all his senses under control. He neither desires for what has not been attained nor grieves for what has been lost.

He who has attained the state of absoluteness, who has realized the supreme self, does not identify himself with body or mind and has no relationship to the work performed by them. He knows for certain, 'I am not the body nor is the body mine. I am consciousness itself'. He does not remember what he has done or not done, for he knows that work pertains to the body and mind and not to the self.

The wise one knows for certain: 'I indeed am in everything, from the highest celestial being down to the lowest clump of grass'. Being ever calm of mind, pure and peaceful, he is free from thoughts and conflicts, and he is free from caring for what is attained and not attained. He does not see anything outside of himself.

The wise one knows for certain that this manifold and wonderful universe is in truth nothing; it is unreal. Thus, he becomes desireless and identified with pure consciousness. Though living in a body and perceiving the apparent existence of the universe, he finds ultimate peace knowing that nothing but the self exists.

Janaka describes his state of self-realization:

I have turned the mind away from dwelling on deeds, words and thoughts, knowing them to belong to the relative plane and not to my true self. Thus, I have become intolerant first of external activities, then of unnecessary speech, and finally of all thoughts. Devoid of all actions, either physical, vocal or mental, I abide in the quietude of my self.

The eternal self is beyond mind and speech; it cannot be an object of perception. When I am firmly established in the knowledge the self, knowing myself and everything to be the one self, then what can I still perceive and through what shall I perceive it? Then what can I still know and through what shall I know it? Free of all attachments, my mind remains one-pointed and empty, abiding steadily in the self.

To the ignorant man, distractions involving people and worldly objects are superimposed on the mind, and he must make an effort to concentrate the mind and inhibit any thoughts that may arise. But to one who is established in the absolute, such attempts at concentration are meaningless. Effortlessly, I abide in the self.

Being the one self, forever perfect and all-pervasive, what would I accept and what would I reject, what would give me joy and what would give me sorrow? Being ever unaffected and unattached I am at peace in my unfathomable self.

Abstention from action is as much the outcome of ignorance as the performance of action. In the eternal self there can be neither action nor abstention from action. Being unattached and beyond action, I firmly abide in my truth.

Of what benefit is it to use thoughts to think of the infinite, the unthinkable? To realize the absolute, I venture beyond all thoughts and become the absolute itself. Unbounded by the mind, free of all thoughts, I firmly abide in my self.

Blessed is the man who through his spiritual efforts has discovered the self, beyond all actions, words and thoughts. But more blessed is he who has become totally dissolved in the self and has become one with the absolute, his own natural state.

The tranquillity that comes when one is firmly established in the self is extremely rare, even for those who have fully renounced the world. One who has realized the self and knows that there is nothing but the self, sees that renunciation, just like attachment, is steeped in relative existence and springs from ignorance. Having given up both attachment and detachment I live happily.

In the struggle to realize the self, the body wearies from doing penance, the tongue wearies from repeating *mantra* and the mind wearies from practicing concentration. Being ever established in the absolute I have no striving and thus live happily.

The true self remains ever unattached and nothing whatsoever is done by it. The body alone acts, owing to its past *karma*. Knowing this, I am not involved with action or inaction and live happily.

Aspirants still deluded by body-consciousness, will be concerned with the activities of the body. Some will insist on the performance of actions to gain spiritual merit while other will uphold the cessation of all actions as the best spiritual practice. But, having no identification with body, mind or senses, and having nothing to gain or lose by actions or inaction, I neither act nor refrain from acting, and live happily.

Who I am is unaffected by what this body does, whether it stays here or goes there, whether it is awake or asleep. No good or evil can accrue to me, whatever happens to it. Therefore, whether the body stays or goes or sleeps, I remain unaffected and live happily.

Good and evil, pleasure and pain come and go. These are qualities associated with the inconstant world; they have no relationship to the immutable self. Those who are of the world strive to do good to gain happiness, and they shun evil to avoid pain. But, I am not concerned with thoughts of good and evil, pleasure and pain. I abide in the self and live happily.

He who is empty-minded by nature, who has no desire for worldly objects and is ever immersed in the consciousness of the self, becomes released from all the effects of his past actions, both good and evil, and therefore, is freed from the cycle of birth and rebirth. As long as his body remains he is casually aware of the world, but he is totally unaffected by it, ever abiding in his truth. Even when asleep he remains awake to the self.

Where are my riches, where are my properties, where are my friends, where is my knowledge, where are the sense-objects to distract me from the self? Where even are the scriptural teachings to point me to the self, when all desire has melted away? Having realized the self, who is the supreme lord and witness, and having become indifferent to both bondage and liberation, I feel no anxiety for emancipation.

The behavior of one who is devoid of doubts inwardly, but who outwardly moves about like any ordinary person, cannot be understood by one who is not like him, for the emancipated one's outer ways are no sure clue to his inner illumination. Under all circumstances he remains the same, ever established in the absolute. To understand such a one you must know your self.

*A*gain Astavakra reiterates the highest teachings leading to knowledge of the self. He enjoins Janaka to remain alert not to fall back into delusion and bondage, for even an instant.

A man whose intellect is free from darkness and passion and is filled with light, realizes the self whenever and however the wisdom teachings are imparted to him by the *guru*. For such a qualified aspirant, even a little instruction casually imparted is enough to awaken him to his truth. But a man of impure intellect who has not prepared himself with the necessary disciplines, is bewildered in trying to realize the self even after seeking self-knowledge throughout his life.

Liberation is nothing more than non-attachment to the illusory objects of the senses whereas bondage is attachment to the sense-objects. This is the essence of all the teachings. It is the recognition of the unchanging non-dual nature of the self, which is the only reality. Knowing this, do as you wish.

Once the self is realized and the truth is known there is nothing more to be attained. Knowledge of the truth makes an eloquent, wise and active person mute, inert and inactive. Therefore, self-knowledge is shunned by those who want to enjoy the world.

You are consciousness itself. You are not the body, nor is the body yours. You are not the doer who performs actions, nor are you the enjoyer or sufferer of the results of actions. You are the eternal witness, forever free. Go about happily.

Desire for what the mind finds attractive and repugnance for what the mind finds repulsive are what keep you bound. But, the mind is never yours. Its characteristics have nothing to do with you. You are changeless. You are pure awareness itself, ever free from conflict. Move about happily.

You are the one self. You are all there is. Everything is within you and you are within everything. You are forever free of egoism and the sense of 'I' and 'mine'. You are the ocean in which all the worlds manifest themselves like waves. Worlds come and go, created by the mind, but you are not affected. Be happy.

Have faith, my child, have faith. Never confuse yourself in this. Be free from the fever of the mind. You are the one reality, the unchanging truth. You are knowledge itself, you are the self, you are the lord, you are ever beyond nature.

The body, like all things of the illusory world, is made up of the five elements. It is governed by the three qualities of nature... inertia, activity and balance. It is born, it stays for awhile and it dies.

The self is eternal and unchanging; it neither comes nor goes. Why, then, do you mourn for this ephemeral body? Let the body last to the end of the age or let it go this very day. How does that affect you? Where is the increase or decrease in you who are pure consciousness and ever free?

In you, the infinite ocean, the universe is like the waves that rise and fall according to their own nature; you, the ocean, are neither enhanced nor diminished thereby. Endlessly, the universe cycles through its stages of creation and dissolution, but you, who are ever beyond time and space, are not affected by its comings and goings. Where then can there be any gain or loss for you, whatever happens to the universe?

My child, you are pure intelligence, you are wisdom itself. When you search out the true basis of the universe you will find it to be your very own self. In reality, the universe is not different from you, for you alone exist. Can gold ornaments such as rings, necklaces and bracelets be anything other than the gold out of which they were made? Are waves anything other than the ocean from which they arose? Completely give up all distinctions. Consider all as the self and be happy.

What can you desire or reject, knowing that all there is is one with you? What can ever be separate from you? What can be born and what can die?

28

Who is there to act or remain actionless? Where is the room for an ego when all there is is you, the one immutable, stainless, pure consciousness?

Through ignorance you conceive a separate universe, but the universe has no existence apart from you. A separate universe is just an illusion; it is nothing. There is no individual self and there is no supreme self other than you, the one self. When you realize this, you become desireless and enveloped in peace.

In the ocean of the world only one ever was, is, and will be. O pure intelligence, do not disturb your mind with affirmations and negations. You have neither bondage nor liberation. Completely give up even the practice of contemplation and meditation. Be calm and contented. Hold nothing whatsoever in your mind. What will you achieve by thinking? What could there still be for you to desire? You are ever free. Abide happily in your own self which is bliss itself.

My child, the self alone exists; all else is unreal. When consciousness of the body or the things of the world engage your attention you cannot abide in the self. The self cannot be known through the intellect. Even filling your mind with the highest spiritual teachings will not lead you to self-knowledge. To realize the self you must forget all.

O dear one, you may strive and be active in the world, you may pursue enjoyment of the things of the world, you may choose to be inactive in the world and engage yourself in various spiritual practices. Whatever you do, your heart will ever yearn to be free of all doings and desires, and to abide peacefully in its own true nature.

All are unhappy because they exert themselves. Exertion presupposes desire, and desire, whether satisfied or unsatisfied, is the cause of all misery. The blessed one may be active or inactive outwardly, but he is ever inactive inwardly, having eradicated all his desires. He abides steadily in the self, completely detached from all mental and physical activities. True happiness belongs to such a master idler in whom even the intentional closing and opening of the eyelids would be an affliction.

When the mind is free from the sense of duty and no longer dwells on the opposites such as 'this is to be done' and 'this is not to be done', it gives up its pursuit of sensual enjoyment and worldly prosperity. It becomes totally indifferent to all desires and life goals. Even the quest for religious merit and liberation are meaningless to it.

One who covets the sense-objects becomes attached to them; one who abhors or renounces the sense-objects becomes non-attached to them. But he who realizes that all is the self, is neither attached nor unattached. For him there can be no thought of accepting or rejecting anything.

As long as the feelings of attachment and repulsion or desire and aversion continue, they becloud your understanding of the true nature of the world. These pairs of opposites stem from ignorance; they make up the roots and branches of the tree of phenomenal life. They delude you into considering the unreal to be real and the real to be unreal.

Activity prompted by desire begets attachment; abstention from activity begets aversion. The man of wisdom is free from all pairs of opposites. He is equally at peace in inactivity or activity. He is playful like an innocent child, free of attachment or aversion for anything.

Thinking that the cause of all sorrow is in the world, you seek to renounce the world to avoid all further sorrow. But it is not the world which is the root of your misery, it is your attachment to it that gives rise to sorrow. When you are fully free from attachment, sorrow cannot touch you. You will not feel miserable even in the world.

If you consider the body as your own, if you are caught up in the sense of *I* and *mine* and harbor egoistic feelings regarding your spiritual attainments, you are neither a *yogi* nor a wise man, but only a deluded sufferer of misery.

Even if the Lord of the Universe were to come and instruct you in the highest teachings, the splendorous self will not shine forth and reveal itself unless you forget all and totally transcend the mind.

*A*stavakra now speaks of the man of abiding wisdom. He describes the characteristics of the illumined one who is a true knower of the self.

Being ever satisfied, with his senses purified, wanting nothing, enjoying being alone, the knower of truth delights in sipping the nectar of the fruits of self-knowledge. Being ever happily absorbed in the self, how can any sense-object attract him or repulse him, please him or displease him?

If a monkey were savoring a grove full of ripe bananas and were delighting in its sweet fruits, would it pay attention to the bitter barks and roots that are also there? Knowing that the whole universe is filled with himself alone and seeing everything as one, how can the enjoyer of the self ever succumb to the pleasures of the senses, which are all attended by misery?

Those desirous of worldly enjoyment and those desirous of liberation can both be found in this world. But rare indeed is the one on whom no impressions are left of things experienced and for whom no desire remains for things not yet experienced. Such is the great-souled one who neither yearns for enjoyment nor for liberation. Totally un-concerned about worldly prosperity, he is neither attracted nor averse to activities or duties. He is even indifferent to whether his body lives or dies.

The blessed one is content with whatever sub-sistence comes to him as a matter of course. With his mind absorbed in the self, he lives happily, whether seeing, hearing, touching, smelling or eat-ing. Being filled with the knowledge of the self, he does not shun the universe or want its dissolution. He sees only the self.

The wise one neither stays awake nor sleeps, he neither opens nor closes his eyes. At all times, in every place he abides in the self, enjoying the su-preme condition. For him the ocean of the world has dried up. Pure in heart and freed from desires, he neither clings nor shuns, he neither slanders nor praises, he neither gives nor takes, he neither re-joices nor frowns.

Devoid of all attachments and disidentified with the objects of the senses, the man of knowl-edge is free of all efforts and non-efforts, though he may be hearing, seeing, touching, smelling, eating, speaking, sitting or walking.

The great-souled one does not become per-turbed by anything. He remains equanimous and self-poised, whether he is seeing a beautiful woman full of love or seeing the approach of death. For him there is no difference between happiness and misery, man and woman, prosperity and adversity.

The knower of the self is neither humble nor insolent, neither curious nor apathetic. Having transcended the limitations of human nature and worldly life, how can he ever cause harm to anyone or even commiserate with another's suffering, when for him there is no other?

Cleansed of the feeling of 'I' and 'mine', with all his inner desires set at rest, knowing for certain that there is nothing separate and that all there is is the one self, the liberated one neither abhors the objects of the senses nor craves for them. Ever with a detached mind he experiences them as they come.

Though he may be acting, the wise one does not act. Being of vacant mind and having gone beyond worldly life, he is not buffeted by the conflicts of good and evil. Nor is he concerned about being in contemplation or non-contemplation. He abides as it were in the state of absoluteness.

To one who is attached to the world, the liberated one's look may appear to be vacant, his actions purposeless, and his senses inoperative, but he is always fully present to the awareness of his own truth. Free from delusion, dreaming, and dullness, he attains an indescribable state in which his mind has melted away, its functions having ceased to operate.

*A*stavakra completes his discourse with a description of the sublime peace that marks the inner state of one who has realized the self:

Salutations to the supreme self which is utter calmness and bliss itself. When knowledge of that splendorous effulgence dawns in the awakened one, all delusion disappears, just as the dream of the night vanishes when one awakens from sleep.

True happiness can never arise from the accumulation of worldly objects, which are invariably attended by fear. Surely one can never be happy without renouncing one's attachment to sense objects and the illusory attractions of the world.

Thinking that the world is real and his actions in it have real value, the deluded person pursues the observance of duty and is scorched by it. How can his sorrow be relieved but by the sweet nectar of tranquillity? The divine bliss and inner peace which is the very nature of the self is always present, regardless of one's activities or inactivity.

The universe is merely a thought, a projection of the mind. It has no existence apart from the self. In reality it is nothing. Being nonexistent it ever remains nonexistent. The self alone is real. Being ever existent it is never nonexistent.

The immortal self is serene, spotless, immutable. It is the absolute, the one reality. Being neither far away nor limited, it is ever attained, shining as your true nature. When all illusions are dispelled, true vision is unveiled and the self is realized. Then all sorrows disappear.

Knowing for certain that the self alone exists, ever free and eternal, would you continue to act like a frightened, deluded child? Knowing that the phenomenal world which appears to actually exist, and that the subtle worlds of visions, dreams and fantasies which do not appear to actually exist, are all figments of your imagination, would you still be affected like an ignorant person?

Once you have become free of all desires, what would be left for you to know, say, or do? All such thoughts as 'I am this' and 'I am not that' would have no meaning when you have become utterly silent, knowing unequivocally that all there is is the self.

To the *yogi* who is unbound and ever at peace, there is no difference in heaven or in beggary, in gain or in loss, in society or in solitude. Having attained control over his senses, his mind is perfectly balanced and tranquil. Neither the practice of concentration nor the gaining of knowledge nor the experience of pleasure or pain can distract him from his equanimity.

Where are the goals of human life, where is performance of ritualistic or meritorious works? Where is worldly prosperity, where is sense-enjoyment? Where are the pairs of opposites? And where even is the practice of discrimination for the wise one who has transcended all dual notions such as 'this is to be done' and 'this is not to be done'?

Where is delusion, where is the universe? Where is renunciation, moreover where is liberation for the great-souled one who rests beyond the world of desires? One who sees the universe and then attempts to deny it is still in ignorance. What has the desireless to do who even as he sees, sees not. For him the universe has no substance or existence apart from the self.

One who has seen the supreme divinity will meditate, 'I am one with that ultimate reality', but what does he who has transcended all thoughts think, when he sees no second? One who sees distraction in himself will attempt to control himself, but what practices are appropriate for the great one for whom distraction has no meaning? Being established in non-duality what has he to accomplish in the world of duality?

The man of knowledge, though living like an ordinary man and appearing to be like him, is totally different from him, for he is not caught up in the illusory values of the world. With his ignorance completely dispelled he abides in the absolute. He lives happily doing spontaneously whatever presents itself.

The wise one feels neither satisfaction nor guilt for what is done or not done. He feels no eagerness in either activity or inactivity. For him there are no duties, attachments or desires of any kind. From the point of view of the world the liberated *yogi* appears to act, for his body continues to be influenced by the effects of his past *karma*. But, within himself, he is totally indifferent to the actions of his body. Without interruption he abides in the pure awareness of the self.

Completely free of all dependence on the world, the wise one moves about like a dry leaf blown by the wind of his past actions. Ever with a serene mind, he lives like one without a body. Having transcended worldly existence, he is neither affected by joy nor by sorrow. With his mind calm and pure, he delights in the self. He has no desire to hold on to anything or to renounce anything.

Naturally of a vacant mind and doing what comes of itself, the wise one, unlike an ordinary man, is not affected by accomplishments or failures, praise or blame, honor or dishonor. Though his body appears to be acting, he does not act, for, in his mind he dwells in his own true nature and knows only the unity of the blessed self.

Though in the world, the liberated man is never attached or bound by it. He is unconditionally happy. Having no distraction he has no need for meditation. Being free of all trace of egoism, his mind is neither troubled nor pleased, but remains actionless, motionless, desireless, and free from doubts. Sometimes he may appear to be acting with reason and purpose and at other times without any apparent reason or purpose. Sometimes he may even seem like a mindless fool. But he is no fool. Having found the ultimate truth, his inner condition is always one of absolute freedom and serenity.

A man who is under the sway of egoism will engage himself in actions mentally, even though he may not take any actions physically. But, the wise one who is free from all egoism, does not engage in any actions mentally, although he may be seen to be acting physically. Being done with all seeking and reasoning he is established in peace, and though in the world, he neither thinks nor knows nor hears nor sees.

The ignorant one aspiring for spiritual merit constantly practices concentration and control of the mind. But he does not attain liberation and lasting peace, either by performing spiritual practices or by abstaining and remaining inactive. The blessed one through merely hearing the truth becomes free. His mind becomes tranquil. Like a person in deep sleep, he does not find anything to be done. Independent of whether his body is active or not, he is happy abiding in the self.

The ignorant person does not attain the absolute, for he desires to become it. He devotes himself to mind control and diverse practices but he does not attain knowledge of that pure, perfect, beloved self which is beyond the universe and beyond all thoughts and practices. As long as he still regards himself as a separate individual existing in a world of individuals and things, he becomes bewildered upon hearing the truth of the self. As long as he is still identified with his actions and practices and considers them as his, he only strengthens the world of illusion and separation.

The wise one realizes the nature of the supreme absolute and attains it even without desiring to do so. On hearing of the self he withdraws within to delight in the self. Knowing the world to be a mere figment of the imagination and the source of all misery, he cuts asunder the very roots of the world by merely being who he is, established in the self.

Where is mastery of the mind for the deluded one who exerts himself to gain control of it? But control of the mind is always natural and effortless for the wise one who delights in the self and whose peace is undisturbed.

Where is self-knowledge for the one who strives to know the self, yet who still sees himself as the seer seeing the seen? The wise one does not see this or that. He sees only his own truth, the immutable self.

There are those who think that the world exists and that the world is real. There are others who think that the world does not exist and that the world is not real. Rare indeed is that blessed one who does not think, but who is ever calm, abiding in the absolute.

There are those who believe that the immortal self is pure and one without a second, but who have not known the self directly and are still caught up in the delusion of the world. As long as they have any attraction or repulsion to the world they remain unhappy and ignorant, despite all their beliefs and strivings.

The one who longs for liberation sees liberation as something outside of himself that he must attain. He ardently practices mind control and concentration, yet he remains in duality, thinking that he is the aspirant and there are practices that he need perform. But the wise one who is totally free from all doubts and whose mind dwells in the self, does not resort to practices to attain liberation. Perceiving everything as one, he is complete within himself.

Knowing the self to be pure undifferentiated knowledge and the only thing worth knowing, the liberated man remains totally free of all desires. Seeing, hearing, touching, smelling, eating, he lives happily.

To the frightened ones who are striving for religious perfection, the sense-objects appear as tigers from whom they must escape at all cost. They seek refuge in the cave of mind control and concentration practices. But to the wise man who is free from desire, the sense objects are like timid jungle creatures who find themselves in the presence of a lion, the lord of the forest. On spotting him they quietly take to their heels. Or, if unable to get away, they serve him like fawning flatterers.

The blessed one in whom self-knowledge has dawned is devoid of all egoism and sense of doership. Rules of behavior do not bind him. His actions are unencumbered like those of a child at play. He does not see what is proper or improper, or prefer either inaction or action. He does freely whatever comes to be done, whether judged by the deluded to be good or bad.

The wise one's conduct is unrestricted by motive and free from all pretense. He shines forth from his very being. The calm of the deluded person is nothing at all like the profound inner stillness of the awakened one. On the surface, the deluded one may appear to be still, but his mind will continue to be attached; and so, he does not shine from within.

Through freedom one attains happiness, through freedom one attains tranquillity, through freedom one attains the supreme. All the modifications of the mind are destroyed when a man realizes that he is neither the doer nor the enjoyer. Ever free from mental projections, unbound and unfettered, he sometimes sports in the midst of great enjoyments and sometimes retires to a mountain cave.

The wise one lives and moves in the self alone. While his external actions continue to be governed by the *karma* that clings to the body, he is not affected. Only those who are like him understand his wonderful state. No desire whatsoever springs forth from his heart. He is not affected whether he is honoring a god or a holy image or whether he is in the company of a great sage or a famous king or a being of exquisite beauty and charm. Nor does he become perturbed when ridiculed or despised by his spouse, children, friends, relatives or strangers. In all situations he remains the same, seeing the one essence in everything.

Though pleased the wise one is not pleased, though pained he does not suffer pain. All such modifications are only of the mind. The liberated one is not affected for he is totally unidentified with the mind. Remaining in perfect equanimity even in worldly life, he is always happy whether he sits, sleeps, moves, speaks or eats. Unidentified with the senses and unattached to the sense objects, he is in the world but not of it.

The awakened one does not differentiate between existence in the self and existence in the world, since for him all is the self alone. He knows himself to be one with that all-pervasive, formless, immutable, untainted self.

Not taking the world to be real, the wise one has no obligation to do anything. Having transcended all sense of duty, he remains unperturbed even while appearing to be engaged in duties. Being pure and childlike, he has no motive in any of his actions. Whatever he does he does without attachment.

For the wise one even action becomes inaction for he has no investment in the fruits of his actions. On the other hand, for the deluded one, even inaction becomes action, since his mind is constantly busy desiring this and rejecting that. Even without doing anything, the deluded one is constantly concerned about duties and agitated by distractions.

Where is the world and where even is the appearance of the world? Where is liberation and where are spiritual practices for the awakened one who sees nothing but himself outside and inside? He is ever changeless; for to him only the self exists. Blessed indeed is that knower of the self who has transcended the mind, who is free from craving, and who, even though seeing, hearing, touching, smelling, or eating, is the same under all conditions.

The deluded one has identified his consciousness with his mind. Believing the mind to be real he is always engaged in either thinking or in trying to control his thoughts by not thinking. But the consciousness of the wise one is ever established in the self. He may appear to be thinking the thinkable but his mind is still and equanimous, empty of thoughts. Knowing that the objects of thoughts are unreal, he remains unattached and free of duality.

The deluded one, after having felt strong attachment for his possessions may become tired of them and experience an aversion to them. But whether it is attachment or aversion, both are associated with the body and are mired in illusion. Where is attachment and where is aversion for him whose love for the body has totally disappeared?

Glorious is he who is free from all desires, who is the perfect embodiment of his own blissful nature and who is spontaneously absorbed in the unconditioned self. Having realized his own self, he does not feel distressed even in worldly life. With all his sorrows permanently gone, he never experiences agitation like ordinary people.

Having realized the truth, this great-souled one neither craves for enjoyment nor for liberation. At all times and in all places he remains free of every manner of attachment. He is perfectly placid like a vast, unruffled lake in the morning stillness. How splendorously he shines!

The pure one to whom the imperceptible self has been revealed, knows for certain that this universe is the product of illusion and that it has no existence of its own. Recognizing the world to be made up of nothing more than changing names and forms devoid of value, he renounces all phenomenal existence and becomes naturally immersed in blissful peace.

What remains to be done by one who is established in pure consciousness? Rules of conduct, dispassion, renunciation, and restraint of the senses — what are all these to one who does not perceive any objective reality and whose nature is the unbounded universal light? For him, the reality of the world vanished with the knowledge of the self.

For one who shines as the infinite where is joy and where is sorrow? Where is bondage and where is liberation? For one who does not perceive relative existence where is the universe, where is the feeling of 'I am the body' or 'the body is mine', and where even is knowledge? For him only a ghostlike illusion of the world remains. Perceiving the self as imperishable and untainted by grief, he is free of any feelings of 'I-ness' and 'my-ness'.

As soon as the man of dull intellect gives up practices such as mind-control he becomes a prey to desires and fancies. Even when hearing the truth he does not give up his delusion of separate existence and duality. Through suppression he may appear to be still and devoid of mental activity, yet attachment and craving for sense-objects still lurk within him.

For the *yogi* who is immutable and fearless and ever free from all sense of duality, what can gain or loss mean to him? For one who does not see the pairs of opposites, where is darkness and where is light? For one who has transcended all spiritual practices, where is forbearance and where is discrimination; moreover, where is fearlessness for such an awakened one?

His work having ceased with the dawn of knowledge, the wise one does not find an opportunity to do or say anything. In ordinary people's eyes he may appear to be doing and saying, but within himself there is not a trace of 'I am the doer' or 'I am the thinker'.

For one who is impersonal and utterly indescribable there is nothing whatsoever. There is neither heaven nor hell. There is not even liberation-in-life. In short, nothing exists in *yogic* consciousness but the one omnipresent self.

The wise one neither longs for success nor grieves at non-attainment. His cool mind is verily filled with the sweet nectar of supreme bliss. He neither praises the calm ones nor blames the wicked. Contented and the same in happiness and misery, he finds nothing to be done. The desireless one neither abhors birth and rebirth nor yearns to perceive the self. Free from joy and sorrow, he is neither dead nor alive. Ever changeless and eternal he is one with the immortal self.

Glorious is the life of the wise one, free from expectation, free from attachment for wife, children or property, free from desire for the objects of the senses, and free from the care of even his own body. Contentment ever dwells in his heart and he lives on whatever comes to him. He wanders about at leisure, resting wherever he is when the sun sets.

Reposing on the foundation of his own being, completely transcending birth and rebirth, the great-souled one does not care what changes come to his body, whether it drops down and dies or rises up and is reborn. He knows that the body, mind and world are illusions superimposed on the self. What happens to them cannot affect him, the immutable self.

Blessed is the wise one who stands alone as the witness. He is attached to nothing. For him there is no second. Being without possessions he moves about at his pleasure. Being freed from the pairs of opposites all his doubts have been rent asunder and all the knots of his heart have come undone.

Glorious is the wise one who is devoid of the feeling of 'mine'. For him a clump of grass or a clump of rocks or a clump of gold are all the same. The whole of nature has the three qualities of activity, inertia and harmony or balance. But for the wise one, the qualities of activity and inertia and their derivatives, attachment, repulsion, pain, ignorance and anger have been completely expunged. He remains ever serene in a state of inner harmony.

Who but the desireless one knows not, though knowing, sees not, though seeing, and speaks not, though speaking? Who is there to stand comparison with the liberated soul who has no desire whatsoever, whose heart is contented and who is indifferent to whatever the world presents? Be he a mendicant or a king, if he is unattached and if he has been freed from all judgments of good and evil, seeing only the one in all, he truly excels among men.

Where is wantonness, where is restraint and where are rules of behavior for one who is established in the self and is the very embodiment of guileless sincerity? Where is determination of truth for one who is ever established in truth? How and to whom can be described what is experienced within by one who is desireless, whose sorrow is destroyed, and who is contented with repose in the self? Being one with the self he is ever beyond description and words.

Not asleep, even when he appears to be sleeping, not dreaming even when he appears to be dreaming, not awake, even when he appears to be wakeful, the wise one is the same under all conditions, the witness of all three states of mind.

Devoid of thought, even when he appears to be thinking, devoid of the sense-organs, even when he appears to be using them, devoid of intelligence, even when he appears to be reasoning, and devoid of any sense of ego, even when he appears to possess it, he dwells in pure consciousness, remaining unidentified with the body and mind.

The blessed one is not distracted even in distraction, he is not meditative even in mediation, he is not dull even in a state of dullness, and he is not learned even though possessed of learning. He is neither happy nor miserable, neither attached nor unattached, neither liberated nor an aspirant for liberation. He is neither this nor that. How can mere words be used to describe the indescribable?

Freed from the idea of action and of duty, the liberated one does not reflect upon what he has or has not done. Praised, he does not feel pleased. Blamed, he does not feel annoyed. He neither rejoices in life nor fears death. He neither seeks the crowded place nor the wilderness. For him there is no praise, no praiser, no blame, no blamer, no life, no death, and no special place. At all times and in every place, the tranquil-minded one is the same, abiding in the infinite bliss of his own true nature.

Janaka makes his final statement, proclaiming the non-reality of all that can be thought of, spoken of or conceived. In a series of questions, Janaka alludes to his own deep repose and points out how that which is real cannot be conceptualized or spoken of. It can only be known by being it.

I have heard from you, great teacher, the pure knowledge of the truth and with your grace I have been able to use that knowledge to extract from the inmost recesses of my heart the thorn of false understandings. All my doubts have been removed.

Where now are the goals of human life and where even is the practice of discrimination? Where is the past, where is the future and where even is the present? Where is space, where is time, and where even is eternity for me, who abide in my own glory?

Where is despair, where is anxiety, where is fear and where even is tranquility and peacefulness? Where are good and evil and the pairs of opposites and where even is non-duality and oneness? Where is dreaming, where is deep sleep, where is wakefulness, and where even is transcendence?

Where is bondage and where even is liberation and knowledge of the self? Where are the holy teachings, where is the mind liberated from the sense-objects and where even is contentment and desirelessness? Where is the nonself and where even is the self for me who am ever existent, ever free, ever unborn, and ever beyond thought?

Where is I and mine, where is this and that, and where are they and theirs? Where is life and where is death? Where is the world and where are wordly relations? Where is forgetfulness and where even is remembrance of the truth for me who abide in my own glory?

Where is distance, where is proximity, where is exterior, where is interior, where is grossness and

52

where is subtlety? Where is the void, where are the elements, where is the body, where are the organs and where is the mind for me who am ever taintless by nature?

Where is the doer, where is the enjoyer, where is cessation of thought or the rising of thought, where is direct knowledge or reflected knowledge, for me who am ever impersonal?

To talk about the goals of life is needless, to talk about *yoga* is purposeless and even to talk about wisdom is irrelevant for me who repose in the self. Where is the *karma* governing the actions of this body, where is liberation-in-life and where even is liberation-in-death for me, the ever un-differentiated?

Where is creation and where is destruction? Where is the end and where are the means? Where is the seeker and where is the sought? Where is the world and where is the aspirant for liberation? Where is the contemplative man and where is the man of knowledge? Where is the soul in bondage and where is the liberated soul?

Where is the knower, where is the means to knowledge, where is the object of knowledge or where even is knowledge itself? Where is anything and where is nothing for me who am ever pure and non-dual by nature?

Where is attachment and where is detachment? Where is illusion and where is transcendence? Where is happiness and where is misery? Where is distraction and where is concentration? Where is joy and where is sorrow? Where is wisdom and where is ignorance?

Where are the spiritual teachings and where are the scriptural injunctions? Where is the disciple and where is the preceptor? Where indeed is the purpose of life for me, who am ever pure and ever actionless?

Where is existence, where is nonexistence? Where is duality, where is unity? Where is activity, where is inactivity? Where is liberation and where is bondage? Where is the world, where is the individual, and where even is the ultimate bliss for me who am ever immutable and indivisible?

What else can possibly be said? How can words express the inexpressible?

Nothing more emanates from me.

Thus, in deep silence, ends the dialogue between Astavakra and King Janaka. The self is all. The self alone is real and nothing else exists. Only in self-realization can life find fulfillment.

Our Other Publications

* **God and His Gospel**
  M.N. Rao

* **The Propheoy : A Novel of Sai Baba**
  Barbara Gardner

* **God Descends on Earth**
  Sanjay Kant

* **Sai Baba Gita**
  Al. Drucker